A LIFESTYLE OF SERVICE

A GUIDE TO STOP DOING CUSTOMER SERVICE AND START LIVING IT

DEWET BOTES

i

Table of Contents

WHY I WROTE THIS BOOK

Service is not something you do; it is something you are. That is the main focus of this book. I wrote this book to give simple guidelines to cultivate a lifestyle of service.

Customer service should be, if not number one on your company's priorities list, at least in the top three. It should be walked and talked. It should be part of everyone; from the MD to the cashier to the temporary worker. This book will give you guidelines on how to imprint this into your heart and mind. From there it will be your task to get the message over to your people.

I have a wealth of customer service knowledge that I gathered in the more than 20 years that I have been working in the service delivery industry. I believe I have been in one of the most challenging service delivery industries in the world, which is IT. The knowledge I acquired needs to be shared with the world. Although I gathered most of the knowledge in the IT industry, there are certain generic concepts that are universal and applicable to all industries.

The purpose of the book is to help companies grow revenue. I do not see myself as a business expert, but I see myself as an expert in one field of business that has the highest revenue generating potential. The aim is to help you grow your customer base which in turn will grow your revenue.

I wrote this book to make the world a better place. Serving customers is not just a money spinner. It has the potential to make a difference in people's lives. Yes you need to get paid for the service you offer to others. That is what business is all about, but the principles in this book have the potential, when applied, to change people's lives.

The idea is to cultivate a lifestyle of service. I want you as reader to start making a difference to the sphere of life you service. Whether you are directly delivering a service to a customer or not, we are all in the line of service somewhere. We serve our spouses, children, family, churches, organizations, schools, sport teams etcetera. *A Lifestyle of Service* will help you do that with excellence and it will help you enjoy it while you're at it.

Customer service has been overcomplicated over the years. I will show you that it's not complicated. There are simplistic tools and methods that can be applied to create excellent results. On the African continent where I have lived all my life, there are challenges unique to Africa, but there are also challenges that are universal. My African perspective will give a new simplistic angle to what service delivery can be.

I wrote this book for educational purposes. I wrote it to educate the reader about service delivery, but it does so in a non-academic style. Instead, it uses practical examples and storytelling.

There are life lessons in this book that will have a positive impact on your personal life, family, friends and the society around you. I want to motivate the reader to make the world a better place through serving others.

WHO SHOULD READ THIS BOOK

This book is for everyone, from the most experienced service delivery manager to the rookie. If you are struggling with managing the delivery of good service in your personal life (yes, we'll talk about that as well) or as a business manager, this book will help you overcome that. It will help you to focus anew on the basics that will ensure better service. If you are new to the service industry, this book will pave the way for you going forward.

You should not read this book in the hope that it will give you a complete Service Delivery Framework (SDF) that can be applied as a de facto standard. You should read it with the idea of gathering principles from my personal experiences that you can apply in your own environment. *A Lifestyle of Service* will help you to cultivate your own personal lifestyle of service.

It has been said that an IT person has as much personality as a doorstop. Ironic as it may sound coming from an IT guy, you should read this book if you want to learn something about relationships.

If you are a technology buff and you are having difficulties bridging the tech-human gap, this book is especially for you. It will help you to cultivate your personal relation skills which is a necessity for *a lifestyle of service.*

Acknowledgements

I want to thank the Professional Speakers Association of Namibia for hosting a conference of international standard in Windhoek. The conference triggered the writing of *a Lifestyle of Service.*

I want to thank Dr Gustaf Gouws for his inspiration and for sparking the idea that I have a valuable contribution to make to Africa and the world, especially in bridging the gap between technology buffs and people.

I want to thank every company, colleague and customer that has crossed my path since 1997. It is through my endeavors with you that I have acquired the content of this book.

I want to thank Marika Bruns for the illustrations and Corne Botes for editing the book.

I want to thank my wife Belinda for a lifetime of support and believing in me for every venture (especially this book) that I undertake. You have made valuable contributions to *A Lifestyle of Service.*

CHAPTER 1. IT STARTS AT HOME

"Service delivery is not an 8:00 to 17:00 job."

LIFESTYLE OF SERVICE

Welcome to *a Lifestyle of Service*. Let me start off by laying a foundation of what this book entails. The golden thread that you will find throughout this book is service as a lifestyle. No matter what line of business you find yourself in, you will be involved in service one way or another. You will either indirectly service your peers, another department or your boss or you will directly service your customers.

Let me tell you a story. One day a position opened up at the company I worked for. I was one of the managers at the company and the vacant position entailed often working in close relationship with the managers. When a close relative of mine applied and got the job, the other managers said they'd have to be careful of the way they conducted themselves, especially towards me. I told them no one's conduct should ever have to change just because someone new was in the office. If that as the case, we should rather analyze our past actions and see if they were pure.

Your actions and your words should be consistent whether you are at work or at church, whether your kids are present or not, whether your spouse is present or not. If you won't say or do something when your spouse, child or pastor is present, then you should probably not say or do it at all.

Service falls in the same category as your conduct. It should be consistent. Service delivery is not something you switch on at 8am when you arrive at work and switch off when you go home at 5pm. If that is the case you will find that delivering good service will be tiresome. It will wear you out. Service will be something you have to force whereas it could be something you do as a lifestyle.

Customer service and good service delivery should not be seen as a slavish act. It is not someone of lower esteem serving someone of higher esteem. In today's world, service is something you offer to someone else that will enrich that person's life. It is something you do, not because you are forced to do it, but because you have offered it out of your own free will and you are getting paid to do it. As long as people are willing to pay me for my services because they are too lazy to do it themselves, they simply don't know how to do it or for whichever reason, you can count me in.

CHARACTER

A lifestyle of service needs to be part of your character. Your customers will have an opinion about your service. Hopefully it is positive. Maybe it is negative. Regardless of their opinions, the reason why your customers have an opinion about your service is because they have dealt with you before. If a customer has not been your customer at least once, how do you convince him of the level of service you provide? How do you sign that first deal? There is advertising and word of mouth and flyers and all sorts of ways to get a customer in your shop. For Leon though from L Barnard Auto & Truck Repairs it was not any of these that got me to use his services for the first time. It was his character.

Leon and his team deliver excellent service at an affordable rate. I take my vehicles from now on go for services to them. They've helped me with anything from a squeak in the engine to a new trailer plug, to a complete engine replacement. My very first dealing with them saved me more than N$4000 on parts alone. I'm not talking knock-offs or pirate parts. I'm talking genuine parts, exactly the same as those sold by the authorized dealer.

Character does not cost you anything. It's a way of life. It is not a mask you put on and take off whenever you feel like it. It is inseparable from you. It is visible at work, on the sports field and in the mall. That is why I went to Leon. The very first time I took my car to Leon, a colleague asked me if he was a good mechanic. I told him I had absolutely no idea. I couldn't vouch for his work. He had never worked on my vehicles before that day. What I could vouch for was his character. That was what got him the deal.

Gaining customer trust is what you do on the job and off the job. It is the way you carry out your duties as president of the neighborhood watch that draws people's trust. You cannot be late every time, not have the previous meeting's minutes ready and not have an agenda. It is the way you coach the grade 5 hockey team. You cannot be late for matches or just play your own kid all the time. It is the way you conduct yourself at the restaurant. Are you shouting at the waiter and being unnecessarily rude? Customers trust people who are of sound character, who are trustworthy and reliable. It is that simple.

HONESTY

A few months back I had to conduct an investigation about items disappearing from a certain location. We got a tipoff, I made a disguised phone call and before I knew it, I found myself sucked into a whole undercover investigation. It required a week long process of pretense and deceit to lure the perpetrators in and set up a sting operation. It is not nearly as fascinating and exciting as in the movies by the way.

It literally made me sick for a day when the whole thing was over. Dishonesty is a sickening thing. It is a dead certain customer relationship killer. Don't get yourself caught up in that. If you have to bribe to get a deal, walk away from it. It's not worth it. Even more so in a small country like Namibia with just about 2.5 million people. News spreads like wildfire. One dishonest deal in the news and you are very likely to lose all your customers. Even the ones you got legitimately.

Some time ago a guy told me about how disgusted he was at the employees of a certain institution in Namibia. He told me his story of when he had to pick up a personal document. He found himself in a room of about fifty people, all waiting to be called by the official clerk behind the counter. He saw how people would walk up to a certain drawer, how they would pull it open, put money into it and a few minutes later this person's documents would magically be handed over by the official. He ranted about the blatant corruption. He was right. It was blatant. I absolutely agreed with him.

But then he continued...He said he stood up, dropped money in the drawer and immediately his documents were ready for collection. Again he ranted on about the corrupt system. Now that is exactly the problem. You will find yourself facing many temptations on a daily basis. You will have the choice to jump into the stream of corruption or to be the daring individual that does not do as everyone else does. I dare you to be the guy who gets the deal without the hunting weekend, all expenses paid add-on, for the person whose signature you need. Do it without the *personal retainer* on the side and without the *sponsor* to the signee's *other business*.

A few years back my brother did a proposal for a rather huge national contract. He had spent weeks on preparations and it finally came down to the time of presentation. I was shocked when he told me what happened right after the presentation during which he had laid out in detail what they could offer and what the savings would be for the specific institution. The project leader of the institution asked him openly, without any regard for others in the boardroom, what they as deciding committee would get out of the deal and specifically what he would gain from it. My brother candidly told him that he and his whole team would get their incentive in the form of salaries every month for simply doing their jobs. Needless to say, that was not well received and my brother did not get the deal.

Whether a customer is willing to do business ethically or unethically, the final decision lies with you. You do not want to deliver any kind of service to an unethical customer. It's bad for your reputation and it's bad for your business. It's not worth the million dollar deal. Walk away from it!

Honesty, coupled with good service, lets you get away with murder when it comes to your customers. When you build up a relationship with a customer and they get used to the level of service and honesty you bring to the party, you will find that the occasional slip-up will be overlooked.

One day a salesperson made a huge cock-up with a proposal. Our office administrator at the time gave him the proposal document to deliver to the customer. All she had to do was add our company profile to the pile of papers. For some obscure reason (obviously by mistake) she stapled the supplier's quotation to the back of the proposal. So it was the salesperson's cock-up in part, because he should have double-checked the document again before delivery, but she had a big role to play as well.

He dropped the proposal off and while he was sitting there the customer paged through the proposal. He suddenly asked the salesperson why there were two pricing structures. Confusedly the salesperson leaned forward and saw the supplier's quotation. He couldn't believe his eyes!

From the supplier's quotation he could calculate our markup to the finest detail. Guess what he said when the salesperson told him with a red face that it was actually our supplier's pricing? He told him exactly just that: *"So I can actually work out exactly what you are making?* At that moment all the salesperson could do was grab the document and run, but he didn't.

The customer's next move was astonishing. He tore off the supplier's quotation and handed it to the salesperson. He told him it was an honest mistake. He said he was not interested in knowing the markup percentages, because history had shown that our pricing had always been within market trends and that our service levels made it worthwhile in any case.

Honesty will let you get away with murder with all your relationships in life, not just with your customer relationships. The supplier quote cock-up didn't end there. A few days later at the office, word somehow got out of what had happened. This was an event that merited potential disciplinary action. Unfortunately, missus office administrator denied any fault on her part, leaving the salesperson out in the cold. He had to take whatever was coming his way. This salesperson though was a guy of impeccable character. He made it out with a mere slap on the wrist and rightfully so. He got away with murder because of his honest character.

TREAT ALL ALIKE

I don't have proof that the following is a true story, but it makes for a good illustration anyways. I heard this story of a customer that walked into a luxury car dealer in Windhoek to do a purchase. He was dressed in flip-flops, dirty PT shorts and a half-buttoned shirt. The salesperson on the floor halfheartedly attended to this customer. He tolerated the guy for about forty minutes as he climbed into every single vehicle on the floor.

The sales person was just about to let this guy know he was wasting his time and that he needed to go when the customer told him he'd take the N$1,200,000 car. He asked him if they accepted cash. The salesperson sarcastically smiled, nodded and waved to the guy as he left. Five minutes later the guy returned with someone looking like what can only be described as a bodyguard, carrying a briefcase with more than N$1,200,000 in cash. The moral of the story is the age old, *don't judge a book by its cover.*

Treating all people the same is not something that comes naturally. We are all rather naturally inclined to treat people differently, depending on who they are or depending on who is around. There are many factors that influence the way we treat people, for example your upbringing, your religious background, your gender, etcetera. If you don't agree with me, think about your behavior around the braai with friends. Would it be different if your boss or the pastor was there? Think about what you are like in the gym. Would you act differently if your wife was with you? Think about the way you look at the beggar at the traffic light versus the CEO of one of your customers.

The challenge lies in changing our perspectives of our customers so as not to discriminate against their gender, race, colour, politics, dress code or anything else. It requires a change of heart and mind to cultivate a lifestyle of service. I can guarantee you that if you lead a lifestyle of service towards all of society, you will find life to be more enjoyable. Change your mindset about service so that it is not this dreadful thing you have to do, but let it become a lifestyle.

You will realize that it actually has life enriching potential for the people around you. You will earn more revenue than your competition, because people will be drawn to the good experience you give them.

> *Service is a lifestyle. It is not something you do. It is something you are.*

CHAPTER 2. DON'T TAKE IT PERSONAL

"When was the last time a customer asked you how you're doing?"

WHO IS IT ABOUT?

Have you heard the joke about the mother-in-law? It is short, but catchy and it goes like this: *Once upon a time, long, long ago, there lived a nice mother-in-law. But it was a long time ago and it was just that one.*

This joke is applicable to the service delivery industry and especially in the IT world. Maybe it is a little exaggerated and generalized, but *mother-in-law* can be replaced with *"service consumer"* (computer user, vehicle owner etcetera): *Once upon a time, long, long ago, there was a nice customer, but it was a long time ago and it was only that one.* You might know what I'm talking about especially if you are an IT technician, mechanic or in any other position where you provide technical services.

When is the last time a customer phoned you and asked you how you're doing and then only told you about the problem they're experiencing? Not lately right? No, it is more likely a case of *my printer is broken again*, even though the last time you were there was 2 months ago. Or *since you serviced my car, my cabin lights don't work*, even though you replaced the breaks.

When you are in service delivery, you need to learn the art of what I call *respectful ignorance*. An angry customer is, more often than not, not attacking you as a person, but rather the situation and frustration he experiences. (If it is an attack on your character and on you personally it is a different story.) The customer might have a deadline or a meeting or some sort of crisis that is important to him and the tool that he needs is not working. Don't take it personally. He has become dependent on you and that in itself is a real frustration for many people. You have to learn to brush it off. In your mind act as if you couldn't care less, yet never show that to the customer. Become respectfully ignorant.

Often the customer needs to blow off steam and once the pressure cooker has done so, things are much better. Again the customer has no right to demean you and you definitely have the right to defend yourself if that is the case. But if you take every call personal you are bound to end up somewhere where the corporate wear is a straightjacket.

You will quite often find that the temperament of the person that makes the phone call to your helpdesk is completely different from the temperament of the person you meet face-to-face onsite, even though it's the same person physically. The phone detaches a caller from the other party. It gives the caller a sense of security and anonymity. It makes him feel safe to talk in a way he would not do otherwise.

Often the customer makes the common mistake we all do of taking action in a time of flared emotions. It makes us say and do things we would not normally say and do. So the customer, being human just like you, in a moment of frustration, phones you and you just happen to be the lucky one on the other end. I'm not being sarcastic by saying you are the lucky one. You really are, because you are presented with the opportunity to grow your personal relationship skills. Don't see it as a problem. See it as a challenge. Grab the bull by the horns and see if you can win the battle.

The battle is won when you have a calmed down or smiling customer. Getting the smile is difficult at this stage. It is easier when you are standing face-to-face with the customer, simply because people mostly do not like face-to-face conflict. That initial phone call is filled with emotion, but by the time you are looking the customer in the eyes, most of the initial flare has subsided.

In the end it is not about you. It is about the customer. Without customers no business can exist. Remember this book is about **service** delivery. Think about the part where you are listening to a raging customer, as one of the services that you offer. Yes, you're not a psychiatrist getting paid to do that specifically, but it is an integral part of the whole package that you deliver. It is part of "fixing" the customer discussed in the next chapter.

I learned the art of *respectful ignorance* when I worked for Document Management Systems (DMS) in Windhoek. Or let me not say I learned it back then as if I now have it down to an art. It is a continuous learning curve. Let me rather say I came up with the idea back then. I realized that to make it in service delivery, I would have to get my emotions sorted out. I can't lose my temper every time a customer behaves completely irrationally. Neither can I lose my temper every time the customer has a legitimate reason for behaving like a lunatic.

Initially it was very challenging, especially when I knew for sure the customer had no grounds for acting the way he did. I worked consciously on this at first, reminding myself continuously about it. When I was about to face a difficult customer I would prepare myself and make up my mind beforehand that I would not lose it no matter what.

At first it took a whole lot of effort. Later on it became second nature to me. Have I now arrived and won't ever lose my temper again with customers, especially the irrational ones? Of course not! But I can count the times it happens now per year maybe on one hand. In the past, even if I was an octopus, I would run out of hands on a monthly basis to keep count.

During my time at DMS I became the sought after person to handle difficult customers. They would literally put the call through to me when the fight started. There were *those* customers that would by default be transferred to me. You know every business has *those* customers? The ones no-one wants to talk to or work with. We'll talk more about *that* customer later. For now I want you to know that it is not about you. It is about the customer. The sooner you grasp that concept the sooner life will be better.

It's About the Customer

I had the privilege of meeting Mike Handcock in 2018 at the Authentic Stage Conference hosted by the Professional Speakers Association of Namibia (PSAN). What an amazing international speaker, rock-star, writer and producer, with a unique shoe style. He wears pointer shoes with these vibrant patterns and colors on them. Not bad Mike, but not necessarily my style!

Mike's talk was called Leadership to Legacy. In his talk he said the following, "Customers do not care about the work you do, but only about the *emotional value* of the outcome

you help them create". The focus is on the emotional value. He actually talked about selling yourself to a customer as a professional speaker. I realized that it is exactly the same in the service industry.

A huge part of "fixing" the customer is attending to their emotional needs. When a customer's problem relates to something IT and it is causing him downtime, he needs to get the problem resolved of course. He needs to get back online. That is his number one priority and rightfully so. For you as the IT guy that needs to provide the solution, it must be your main priority as well. Yet the road to the final delivery of the solution involves a great deal of emotional selling. It involves reassurance and putting the customer at ease. It involves attending to him quickly. It involves proper communication - keeping him in the loop all the time. It involves delivering on your promises.

On the other hand, it does not involve you boasting about how good you are and how the customer can be glad that you're actually the one on site. Yes, I've heard IT technicians actually saying that. It definitely also does not involve you trying to sound smart by throwing in all the IT lingo into the conversation. Let me tell you a secret. One of the easiest things to do is to sound smart among non-IT guys. They mostly have no idea what you're talking about after the first hello. That's like me when a mechanic tries to explain to me what is wrong with my car. I know nothing about engines. They lose me after the first mention of a *carburetor, piston, manifold* or some other car part. So stop it.

It's not about you. It is about the customer. It is not the guy that appears the smartest that will be called next time. It is the one that can relate to the customer. The one that can disarm the situation. Explain to him in normal English what the problem was and how you fixed it. That forms part of the whole experience and the emotion the customer has. The smart talk is not what will get you the job next time. It's the fact that you sold the customer a pleasant emotional experience (actually providing the solution obviously goes hand-in-hand with it). It is the fact that you didn't make it about yourself, but about the customer.

There are several tricks that you can use to make the customer feel special. Let me just touch on a few of them that are low hanging fruit giving you the quickest gains. The first one, I have to admit, I learned from my wife. She runs her own online retail shop where she sells handbags and other ladies' accessories. She's been building up her database of customers over the past 4 years. She would save every single customer on the contact list of her mobile. All the names would start with *ERIKAS* (the name of her business is Erika's Handbags) followed by the actual name of the customer. You can image the size of her contacts list.

Needless to say, her contacts list is her holy grail and rightfully so. It needs to be backed up regularly and synced to Google, MS OneDrive, Dropbox and the Samsung cloud. I feel sorry for her poor IT guy. He really has his hands full with everything. She has 24/7 access to him, knows where he lives and what he's doing all the time. But they really have a special relationship.

To get back to my story, what I learned from my wife is the power of personal touch. She says she can hear the surprise in a caller's voice if she answers the phone with a "*Hi there, Michelle*"or a "*Good morning Christine*", especially if they've had only one dealing in the past or if it has been weeks since they last spoke. We all like hearing our own names. It is even more so when we don't expect it.

In March 2018 I did my first Two Oceans Marathon in Cape Town. Alright, I attempted my first Two Oceans Marathon. (How significant is 3 minutes really?) I remember how surprised I was every time someone in the crowd would go, *"You can do it, Dewet!"* or *"Keep going, Dewet!"* Remember Cape Town is not in Namibia where I live. The first few times I almost sprained my neck to see who was shouting my name. It was just so amazing. Here I am in another country, doing my first marathon and people are actually recognizing my face?! They called me by name! But then I remembered...our names were actually printed on our race numbers.

Hearing your own name gives you a good feeling. Your customer will feel much better if you say *"Good morning, Ann* instead of just *"Good morning",* because you acknowledge her personally.

You need to gather personal information about your customer and use that in your dealings with him. If you know they support the Springbok rugby team and they won over the weekend, talk about that during your Monday visit. Record their birthdays so that when you happen to talk to them some time close to the date, you can wish them a happy birthday. Don't phone them on the day to congratulate them. To me personally that is just weird, because you are not friends.

Ask them about how their son did in the golf tournament or their daughter in the dance contest. You gather this info as you build the relationship with the customer. Gather the info as you stumble upon it while overhearing a conversation, for

example. It can also be information that you gathered during a previous conversation. Don't go Google and Facebook a new customer and then ask him about his dad's birthday party the previous night. That is inappropriate and you might once again find yourself in that place where your corporate wear is a straightjacket.

So you have gathered some information you can use to connect with the customer on a personal level, but then there is the actual moment you meet face-to-face. Here you simply stick to basic human behavior and interaction principles. Consider proper cellphone etiquette. Don't walk into a customer's office while texting or reading an email or even, heaven forbid, talking on the phone. Make eye contact. Walk up to the customer with confidence. Maintain eye contact as you do a firm handshake. Firm handshakes speak of confidence.

The first impression is very important. Remember that first impressions already start during the initial phone call. So don't answer the phone like you're the owner of the fast food outlet around the corner. Be professional. Don't do the auctioneer-speed Hi-This-Is-ABC-Company-Mary-Speaking-How-Can-I-Help-You thing. Have you ever noticed that nine out of ten times a caller that is greeted this way ends up asking if he is now indeed at ABC Company or asking who is speaking? The names are just completely lost in all the gibberish. Speak clearly. Speak slowly enough.

Then there is my personal favorite. You are bound to get this at least one out of five times in Namibia. It goes like this:

> Operator: Hello.
> Caller: Hi. Is Brian there?
> Operator: Yes...(and then silence)

The operator goes quiet, because he has answered the question. The caller goes quiet, because the next obvious step would be being transferred to Brian. Following the few seconds of silence, the operator would then knock the caller out with something like, *"Yes sir, can I help you?"* The important thing here is teaching your reception personnel basic phone etiquette. Your reception should sound enthusiastic. The customer should be left with the impression that this company wants to talk to him and wants

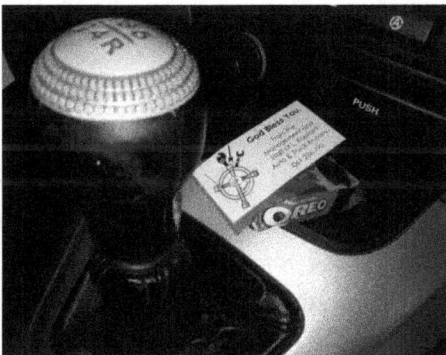

to help him. If you are not delivering funeral services, don't sound like you're among the dead.

You don't have to do the proverbial pulling a rabbit from the hat every time you serve a customer. Often a small gesture to show appreciation works even better magic. This is what L Barnard Auto & Truck Repairs in Windhoek does. It is simple, but effective. Whenever they service your car, you get a small thank you note attached to a packet of Oreo cookies. It leaves you with a warm heart and it costs Leon and his team basically nothing. The warm heart is just the means to an end, because Leon is not in the business of making people feel warmhearted. He offers mechanical services, but the warm heart is what makes people bring back their vehicles.

IT IS ABOUT OTHERS

In Windhoek we have 6,492 taxis with a population of 325,000. This equates to 50 people per taxi. Compared to other cities in the USA we see New York has 154 people per taxi, Chicago has 400 per taxi and Detroit has a staggering 667 people per taxi. Compared to these cities, which by the way have other means of public transport available as an alternative, we see that Windhoek has the highest number of taxis per capita, with only a few busses as alternative public transport. So, it is needless to say that Windhoek's infrastructure and road network face a challenge in this area. It is evident every day during rush-hour traffic.

Every day I see taxi drivers and private car owners going deaf instantly. I know this because I see them switch over to sign language the moment either party thinks the other party has offended him in some way. There is an overuse of one finger especially. But that is not what I want to focus on. I'm focusing on customer service.

Apart from taxis in Windhoek, I have never experienced another industry more focused on customer service. It's not just in Windhoek. I cannot vouch for your city, but I have heard that globally this is mostly the case and I have experienced it firsthand in Johannesburg, Cape Town, Dar es Salaam, Gaborone and Mauritius.

Taxi drivers are just another species altogether. They GO to their customers wherever their customers are. It is irrelevant whether they are in the far right lane and the customer is in the far left. They stop where the customer is, irrespective of the no-parking or no-stopping sign. They stop when it's green and go when it's red, all for the convenience of the customer.

Understand me correctly. I'm not condoning their actions in the light of good customer service. In fact, I'm not sure whether they do what they do from a customer service perspective or from a never-minded attitude. Irrespective of their reason, I believe that service delivery has a societal connotation. Your lifestyle of service, whichever way you define that, has an impact on the people around you.

Excellent service delivery is crucial for any business, but it should not be at the expense of something or someone else. Don't confuse it with plain old healthy intercompany competition. Competition between companies and departments is good. A business needs to take market share from their opponents and compete with quality, pricing, services, value, etcetera. That is not what I mean by "at the expense of" someone else. It rather means the service you offer should not be to the detriment of another. The taxi that speeds, does dangerous maneuvers, parks illegally and suddenly stops in the middle of the road is an example of doing something at the cost of another.

Providing a service should never be at the cost of another individual. That is what is called disservice. It is often the case within an organization as well. People tend to disservice others so that they can rise above them. They try to alleviate themselves above their peers, which in itself is a noble act, yet they do that not by uplifting themselves through harder work or education. They rather discredit others and push them down. That way they seem at a higher level than their peers. Yet they have not grown at all.

In the beginning of the book I give reasons for writing this book and I mention that service affects every part of your life. It is all about balance. You cannot serve your employer to the extent where you neglect your family. You cannot serve your children to the extent where you neglect your wife. Likewise you cannot give your best customer the type or level of service that is detrimental to your business or harmful to others.

The taxi driver cannot swerve from the far right lane over to the left, cause a pileup and run over a cyclist to pick up a customer and then smile about his high service delivery level. A lifestyle of service does not have you at the center of it all. It has someone else at the center. It is about serving another.

I met a guy briefly about 10 years ago in Klein Windhoek. Our paths crossed unexpectedly that day. I cannot remember what he looked like. I won't recognize him today, but I will never forget the look in his eyes that day when he lost everything. I was waiting for my wife outside the store. It wash rush hour and I saw a man carrying a 10kg TopScore Mealie Meal pack. He wanted to cross the busy road and he was ducking and diving cars to get to the other side.

Suddenly he had a gap and he started walking. The next moment a car came around the corner at a high speed. The guy was startled and in the process of jumping out of the way, he dropped the 10kg maize on the road. As the maize hit the road, creating a big white cloud of maize dust, I could see the look in that guy's eyes. At that moment he was devastated as he felt he had just lost everything. Whether this mealie meal was food for his family for the rest of the month or whether this was to run his business for the next few days, I don't know. Nonetheless, his plans had just literally gone up in a white cloud and cars were driving over what was left of it.

At that very moment I was presented with an opportunity to grow my lifestyle of service. Right there I had to make a decision to either walk away from a situation that had absolutely nothing to do with me, or to reach out and help a fellow human being in need. I took him into the store and bought him a new 10kg pack of mealie meal. The joy in his whole being was just overwhelming. It was so much worth my while.

Cultivating a lifestyle of service will sometimes cost you something, but it will empower you and give you tools that you can apply in your business where you can charge money for the services you provide.

> **Service is never about the one who provides the service (you). Service is always about the one receiving the service (others).**

CHAPTER 3. FIX THE CUSTOMER

"A smiling customer is a returning customer"

TECHNICAL VS RELATIONAL SKILLS

During my 14 years at Bytes Technology Group Namibia (BTGN) I gathered a great deal of my customer relationship and service delivery skills. At BTGN we provided a wide variety of IT services to a wide variety of sectors. Our customer base included everyone from national banks, to government and corporates, right down to SME's and sole-proprietors. To give you a brief history about BTGN, it was several strands of previously independent IT companies that were joined under one umbrella through acquisitions. The strand I came from went through three acquisitions before we found ourselves in stable waters that is, to this day, still known as BTG Namibia.

When I started out as a young IT tech, I thought that if I could fix the most devices (PCs, servers, printers etc.) within the least possible time, I'd be the best. I thought that to be able to do that, I would have to be the most knowledgeable in my team. I definitely would have to know more than the customer, but that was easy, because IT guys are the "clever" guys, aren't they? Let me tell you a secret, they're not. They just seem clever when it comes to technology, because the general public is clueless about it. Or at least it used to be like that 20 years ago. Nowadays it has changed quite a lot where everyone, from the farmer to the cleaner, knows about and/or uses technology in some way or another. So I knew I could outsmart the customer easily, yet I had to gather real knowledge in order to outsmart my peers.

Fixing the customer was not on the top of my priority list. Fixing the piece of hardware was. Hit and run was the agenda. Quick in and quick out. If I could spend as little time as possible with the customer, it would be great. The stigma that IT guys, or *propeller heads* as they're sometimes called, have no personality, fitted me perfectly. If the customer expects of me not to be this flamboyant character walking into his office, then that's what they'd get.

I soon found myself at the top of my game. I had done the training. I had read the books. I became the sought after tech to solve a problem. Not the very best always, but good enough to stand out. Come to think of it, maybe I was not that smart after all. Maybe it was more a case of *In the land of the blind, the one-eyed man is king.* During that time of my life, there was not much competition in the group of colleagues I was surrounded by. It's not that my colleagues were clueless. In fact, they were all experts in their fields, but they were all very much technically minded from years of working on very mechanical equipment. The digital age of printers and photocopiers starting to emerge during those years and IT, which was my field, was becoming more and more relevant.

On the one hand, my technical skills were not bad and my IT skills were big, but on the other hand, my customer relation skills were completely underdeveloped. I could fix any piece of hardware, remove any virus and recover any data, but I could not necessarily fix the customer. Getting the piece of hardware to work was my top priority. Service was a minor sideshow. It was one of those by-the-way things that I had to do. I was lightyears away from service being a lifestyle.

More often than not fixed hardware equates to a fixed customer, but that is not always the case. Sometimes it is possible to *fix* the customer without fixing the hardware. Therefore, developing your relational skills are just as important as developing the skills you need to actually do the job. This is true not just in the IT world, but in every business sector you find yourself in.

Can I Develop my Customer Relations?

Brain profiling! What a fun exercise to do at first, but then it gets tedious. There are just too many questions and I'm sure some of them are duplicated. Or maybe it only seems that way. Maybe that is part of the whole exercise. At first you think you can manipulate a brain profile to fit a certain job criteria. They give you possible answers where not one relates to you, but you have to pick one. They make you think about who you are. They make you think about how you would react in different situations. Then they make you wonder if you have not thought about this question already.

And then…everything is blurred. These are dangerous people putting these things together…Psychologists. (And how does that make you feel?)

One of the biggest firms in Namibia and my employer in 2004 did such a brain profile on me. The result was that I was equally "yellow-brained and red-brained". In short, that means I am a problem solver and a people person. The problem with a brain profile is the label it hangs around your neck. The whole company did the brain profiling and it became a culture in the corridors to pin these colors to people's actions.

When a *blue-brain* would suggest looking at the figures one more time before making a decision, someone would say you are overthinking it. When I (*red-brain*) said we cannot make this decision because it would have a negative impact on the staff, I would be told my oversensitive red-brain is too emotional.

What is even worse, is that people were not appointed in a position because it did not fit their brain profile, without being given the chance to proof themselves. That to me is the main disadvantage of brain profiling. It is a remarkable tool to use to see if a candidate fits the immediate requirements for a certain position, but it is detrimental if it labels the individual. It limits a person's potential for growth, firstly from the perspective of the employer, because the candidate is pre-conceived as incapable of filling a given position. Secondly, from the perspective of the employee as he potentially handicaps himself. People don't give themselves a chance. They think that they're unfit for the job, because the brain profile has spoken.

The question therefore is: Can I develop my customer

relation skills? If the brain profile says I have nothing going on in the red quarter, is it possible for development to take place in this red zone? The answer is an undeniable yes! I am living proof of that. If I had done the brain profile back in my early tech days, it would surely be far less red. I did not like engaging with people back then. I have developed though into what I believe to be equally tech savvy and people savvy.

If you want to advance in any environment that has any level of service at its core, it is no more a question of IF you can develop your people skills. It's a case of you HAVE to do it. Remember that it is possible. You might be the *blue-brain* now, but you can change that. Now don't think any one of the quarters are more important than the others. We are all unique. We are all created with an inclination to one quarter more than the others. Certain characteristics in us will always be the dominant ones, but we can grow and cultivate other characteristics as well. You can definitely cultivate a lifestyle of service.

Previously I mentioned Mike Handcock whom I met at the PSAN conference in Windhoek, but someone else I had the huge privilege of meeting was Dr. Irena Yashin-Shaw. In her book, *Leading in the Innovation Age*, she talks about developing technical and leadership skills. She uses an illustration of the earth to talk about the relationship between these skills.

The outer layer of the earth is where everything happens, but the earth's core is what influences the things happening on the outer layer. The molten lava inside the earth is what shapes the surface when it erupts to form mountains. The important thing is that the core can be cultivated and adapted and grown. As it develops, the outcomes on the outer layer change. The conclusion is that the leopard (YOU!) can indeed change its spots (develop other brain profile quarters).

The benefit of developing your relational skills is not just for better customer service. It is for your own personal benefit as well. A few years back I worked in a department of only four technical guys. One of my colleagues was a new guy, but the other two were older than me and had more technical expertise than I had. Both had more experience and both were longer at the company than I was. When the technical manager of our department resigned, he had to be replaced and it was time for one of us to be promoted. The promotion was offered to me and not because of my technical skills alone. It was because of my people skills. What counted in my favor was the fact that I could relate better to people.

Don't get me wrong. You need to know how to do your job. You must always strive to be the best at what you do. Early in my career I went through 3 acquisitions and every time colleagues were retrenched around me. Every time I kept my job because of my technical expertise. Get the balance right between your knowledge about your field of expertise and your relational skills, especially if you are technologically minded. Us propeller heads are not naturally inclined towards people relations.

Proper communication does not just entail verbal communication, but also written communication. Technical guys (especially millennials) think nothing of it when they write an email with smileys and *LOLs* and *gr8ts*. That is unprofessional. If you have to, take a business writing course. Attend an effective communication workshop. Do something like an IELTS test so you have an internationally recognized rating that you can attach to job applications, especially if you are seeking employment abroad.

HOW TO FIX THE CUSTOMER

Once upon a time there was an IT technician. Let's call him Dewet just for the sake of the story. He worked for a company in Windhoek and on this particular day he had to go and sort out a customer's IT problem at her office. It was a very basic IT problem of not being able to scan from her newly purchased multifunctional device (scanner, copier, printer, fax) to her laptop. Dewet arrived at the office finding only the receptionist and the owner's ten year old boy there. The receptionist led him to the laptop and reiterated the problem which was: The boss only wanted to scan to her laptop.

So the arrogant young technician went into his knight-in-shining-armor mode and jumped to work knowing, exactly that the nifty little device got all the bells and whistles when it came to MFPs (multifunctional devices). He inserted ink cartridges and installed every single feature that the machine could offer. He even showed off to the ten year old boy showing him the print quality of the device, as if our arrogant tech had built it himself. He had a bit of a challenge here and there, but he was done in forty minutes, got the job card signed and off he went, happy about a job well done. He had not just fixed the problem, he had over-fixed it!

About an hour later a furious customer phoned our hero. Her ten-year-old boy had basically halved a color ink cartridge by printing literally fifty-something superhero pictures on the printer. The printer was meant as a gift to one of her top customers at a gala dinner that same evening. Weird situation, but she only had the OK from her customer to scan a very important document and mail it off to him! This is the end of the story and unlike all other stories, our young hero did not win the heart of the girl this time. On the contrary, the girl lived unhappily ever after.

If you haven't realized the obvious yet, that was a true story about myself. The mistake I made was to fix the problem and not the customer. The repercussions of my actions were firstly a furious customer who did not want to have anything to do with the company I worked for. The problem is that the actions of an individual (your technicians, frontline staff, team members, sales representatives, receptionist etcetera)

is what create disgruntled customers, but the company is the one that pays for it in the form of lost revenue. Secondly, the initial forty-minute-job could potentially have taken twenty minutes. There you have another loss of revenue. Finally, this type of scenario often calls for a second attempt to go back to fix the customer.

Let me tell you a secret: It is possible to fix a customer without fixing the problem the customer has. How is that possible you may ask? It is done through leaving a customer smiling. This can be done in many different ways, but the *goose that lays the golden eggs* is **communication**. If I, instead of playing knight-knight, had merely communicated to my customer, telling her what the MFP can actually do and that I could configure it all for her, I would probably have "won the girl's heart".

Lack of communication also creates a gap that keeps the customer in the dark. The frustration of a customer not knowing what's happening is detrimental to any business. A smiling customer is one that knows exactly what the next move will be. There are no surprises. He knows he's going to wait X minutes and it will cost Y dollars. When I worked at Bytes Technology Group Namibia, my managing director (JC Kruger) used to say: *We don't give surprises and we don't like surprises.*

Nobody wants to be kept in the dark not knowing what's happening. The frequency of your communication should be of such a nature that the customer never gets the urge to phone you. You should always be the first one to phone him/her with the latest updates. Be transparent about the stock that will not be arriving the next day. Be transparent about the part you ordered which is only due for arrival next week. Tell the customer about any potential risk. Do not oversell on promises. Always build in a time buffer or cost buffer. Life is full events beyond our control. Life is full of surprises. A sudden spike in pricing or delayed delivery date is a surprise and so is a lower price or an earlier delivery date. The difference though is obvious; one is a bad surprise and the other is a good surprise.

Just think of which of these two surprises you would prefer. Think about how you feel when you are made promises and they don't come to pass. Think of the feeling you get when your local telecoms provider promises you for the umpteenth time that they will be there just now. That is the feeling you should prevent your customers from having over you.

WHAT IF I SCREW UP?

There is not a single perfect person, company or process in this world. That unfortunately includes you.

A while back my wife organized a teambuilding function for my son's hockey team. They booked a date and time at a bowling alley. She asked them if they served food or any form of snacks. They mailed her pictures of the platters they make two days before the event. She made her decision and everything was good to go. The bowling alley confirmed everything.

On the day of the event, 3 hours before the scheduled time my wife phoned to confirm if everything was set. To her surprise, the lady on the phone (different to the one through whom the booking was made) knew about the booking, but didn't know anything about platters. She said they don't even do platters. Upon telling her about the photos mailed to my wife and the email confirmation she had, the lady investigated and saw that they had indeed sent a second mail after the initial confirmation. This mail explained that they don't actually cater for meals. The problem was they didn't send it to my wife's address, but to someone else's. So the initial lady made a mistake by offering platters. They actually make use of a caterer from whom the customer can order platters directly.

Up to this point it was an honest mistake on their side. One of their staff members were confused about procedure and it could happen in any company. Their second mistake was not making sure they used the correct email address. Again something that can happen to anyone. That is completely understandable.

It was what they did next that caused real damage to their brand and reputation. What they did about it was...absolutely nothing. My wife said it was fine, but insisted they fix it. Five

minutes later a very confused caterer phoned my wife and they had to resolve the whole matter between the two of them. The bowling alley had made a mistake, twice, but then they did the inexcusable by simply walking away from the problem and passing it on to someone else. That someone else was not just the caterer, but also the customer.

If you screw up (and you will, guaranteed), you go out of your way to fix it. You pull out all the stops. You don't go the extra mile; you go the extra ten miles. You do whatever it takes to resolve the issue, irrespective of whether it is within the normal scope of services you deliver or not. You fix the customer in whichever way necessary. It is alright if you screw up. It is inexcusable if you don't apologize for it. It is completely inexcusable if you don't fix it.

> *Fixing a customer does not necessarily mean resolving his/her problem immediately. Fixing a customer means always leaving him/her in a state of contentment.*

CHAPTER 4. FIRST TIME RIGHT

"Why is there never enough time to fix it the first time around, but always enough time the second time around?" – Carl Sass

MANAGING YOUR TIME

Things in our world today have become busier than ever. On a daily basis we hear the older people saying *time flies*. As we grow older it becomes a bigger reality for ourselves every day. I couldn't believe the date-of-birth on a resume that ended up on my desk a few months back. The date was the same year I finished school. I immediately had a negative feeling about the resume. It's not that I felt the person was too young. It was that I immediately thought there was an error on the resume. No-one born in 1996 is old enough to work and there is absolutely no excuse for making a typo on a resume. I believe you can fail at many things in this world, but a resume should be flawless. A resume is a piece of paper where you sell who you are. There is no room for errors. So I had a negative vibe about the resume because of the supposedly erroneous birthdate! Then it dawned on me: there was actually no error there. This person was indeed old enough to work. He was twenty-two years old and yes, that is how long ago I finished school!

We are living in an instant world where everything happens at the push of a button. I have become ever so busy in my life and I just never have time. Sounds familiar?

I am too busy has become an acceptable phrase in the workplace. Well, I believe it is an evil saying that we have to start managing properly in our personal lives. It has given us an excuse for procrastination. It has become an excuse for inadequate service and basically any other area of failure.

This has definitely become an excuse in the service delivery industry. *I didn't have enough time* has become what I call a cancer in the customer service sphere of things. (There is another cancer called procrastination, but more on that in another chapter.) This has led to the very relevant question of: *Why is there never enough time to fix it the first time around, yet there is always enough time to fix it the second time around?*

In my earlier days as a technician working in the high-volume photocopier and printer industry, this was the cancer of my time. Initially I was part of the cancer. We would consider a call that came back within a determined number of days or within a determined number of prints, to be a call-back. It was one of our key performance indicators that we were measured on.

My own personal best explanation for any call-back was that we were too busy during that specific time that the call was attended to. Or my colleague was on leave and the workload was too heavy. This excuse was specifically effective when even the boss knew it was during a hectic time. I got away with it every time.

I didn't manage my time. The result of this was that I started targeting only the specific problems the customers had. You do quick-fixes on a hit and run basis because there is another customer waiting. You are a busy man and people need you!

The problem is that more than 70% of these quick fixes end up in call-backs.

You need to manage your time in such a way as to allow enough time to fix problems the first time around. There are always exceptions to the rule. You will have call-backs, guaranteed. But when you do, it should be as a result of pure coincidence or something completely out of the ordinary. It should not be because of a second grade quick-fix.

There is this myth that quick-fixes create more time. A quick quotation or proposal enables me to get more quotations and proposals out to customers. A quick solution to my customers' needs will enable me to attend to more customers on my waiting list. The problem is that on a short term basis there is a false sense of *time creation*. In the long run though, you shoot yourself in the foot because the next day you will have to attend to the waiting list of the day AND you have to attend to the call-backs of the previous day. The time you created in theory comes back to bite you in reality.

The call-back concept usually relates to service delivery environments where a physical service is delivered by, for instance an IT technician, vehicle mechanic or appliance repair person. But the concept is applicable to any form of customer service, from sales personnel to merchandisers to cleaning personnel. Call-backs have reputational, financial and morale implications.

CALL-BACK? SO WHAT?

In a technical hands-on environment, customers obviously rely on you as the repairman. These types of physical services usually require some sort of formal training or apprenticeship. The repairman is seen as an expert in his field. There is nothing worse than a repairman who has to return two or three times to fix the same problem. The customer initially loses faith and trust in the person, but later on also in the company.

You will find in any service company you have customers that want only a specific guy to work on their equipment. It's the guy that always fixes the problem. I have seen this at every single service company or department I was involved with. Customers quickly identify favorites. The opposite is also true. Often a customer might tell you that they don't want a certain person to attend to them again. There might be different reasons like personality clashes and others, but mostly customers respond like this because the specific guy didn't fix their previous problem. I've even had customers telling me they would rather wait an hour or two for their regular technician than having anyone else attend to it.

The reputational damage caused by a quick-fix can be devastating. A few years back a delegation of 4 persons from Germany came to Namibia to start a huge cement plant, known as Ohorongo Cement today. We got word of it and we offered our IT services. They set up a small temporary office in Windhoek just to start off with. It was literally a two-room office where they needed 4 network points between the two rooms. The project manager (doubling as acting MD) was in a hurry and they confirmed to me in an email that they didn't care what it looked like. As long as they didn't trip over wires they were fine. I delivered the quick fix they asked for.

Basically overnight their operations grew and the project took off. More people were employed and a permanent MD was appointed. Immediately on arrival, the new MD called me in about the bad job we had done with the network cabling. My explanations were in vain and no email proof helped. The company I worked for had lost all face-value in their eyes and we lost all opportunities to supply IT services and infrastructure for a huge Windhoek head office and a cement plant up north. The new MD literally told me they would never use us again and they didn't. I learned a huge lesson that day. Quick fixes cause immense reputational damage to you as a person and to the company you work for.

The financial implications of call-backs are huge. A bad reputation needs to be fixed. That takes additional man hours to fix. It takes negotiating and extra hard work. It takes far more effort than just keeping a customer satisfied in the first place. If you don't fix it, you end up having to find a new customer to make up for lost revenue. Harvard Business Review posted an article that says it is 5% to 25% more expensive to get a new customer than to retain an existing customer. A further shocking statistic is that a 5% increase in customer retention rates equates to a 25% to 95% increase in profits! You can simply just not afford to deliver bad service. You can just imagine how much revenue we lost with the Ohorongo deal that claims to have made a N$ 3 billion total investment thus far in Namibia.

It is a rather simple principle: We don't go back to where we were mistreated. My wife will never again make use of a certain green courier to get her stock into the country after her bad experience. I will never take my vehicle back for a service to the specific mechanic when the wheel fell off, right after they worked on the CJ joints. You will never go back to the restaurant with the bad service and food. Don't expect your customers to act any different.

TIME = MONEY

Morale and self-esteem also suffer under callbacks. A technician in my team was one day literally in tears when he had to go back a third time to resolve an issue. I accompanied him the third time for two reasons. We firstly needed to do reputational repairs. We had to restore faith in the mind of the customer. That is faith in the technician so that the customer would allow him to work on his equipment again and faith in our company that we take call-backs seriously. Always remember it doesn't matter how harsh you discipline the employee that screws up or how sincere you are about fixing your bad reputation, if you don't take action that is visible by the customer, it doesn't help anything. You have to meet with the customer after a bad experience to restore the relationship.

The second reason why I accompanied the technician is just as crucial. I had to build up the young technician's self-esteem. He was a very technologically promising individual. This was a single occurrence that could potentially destroy his ambition. It was another opportunity for me to serve someone else. We went systematically through the troubleshooting process so as to not overlook anything. I guided the technician. I didn't do the repair myself. In the end he fixed the problem.

> *First-time fixes are always possible and pay well. Second-time fixes are always possible but pay poorly.*

Chapter 5. THAT Customer

"Who wants the swine?"

WHO IS THAT CUSTOMER?

We all have a Mister D (real name omitted for anonymity) on our customer list. We all have him, but none of us wants him. It's the guy that is just never happy. He is never satisfied with anything. He hardly greets you when you walk into his office. Guys like these did not get out of bed on the wrong side; I think they were born angry. Do you know who I'm talking about? Has your Mister D popped up in your mind yet? THAT's the customer I'm talking about.

In my Xerox Namibia and DMS days, we had weekly meetings to discuss call statistics, challenges and potential problem areas. We would also use the opportunity to distribute that day's calls between the technicians. And if Mister D was on the list they would say, "*Who wants the swine?*" He was considered to be the swine (German for pig) in the group. This guy had absolutely no chance of ever being liked by our group. We had pinned swine to his name and that is what he would remain. I'm not excusing myself from the group. I was right there on top of the swine-wagon. Sometimes I was holding the reins!

As it worked out, every now and then I was the lucky winner of Mister D's call. Every time I dreaded going there. It was not just Mister D's eloquent character that one had to deal with. He also had a Great Dane. This was the greatest of Great Danes. This dog, as big as a horse, was more intimidating than Mister D himself.

On one particular day my opinion about Mister D made a 180 degree turnaround. On that particular day I met his son who was autistic. I had not been aware that he had an autistic son before that day. I had also not been aware of the fact that some of the most important rules when raising an autistic child were routine and discipline. It is about controlling the environment for your child. It didn't dawn on me that day, but only later on when I read up on autism.

Mister D was not the swine we made him out to be. He was far from that. He was leading a life of routine and absolute discipline. Meanwhile it was a couple of immature and uninformed technicians that unnecessarily perceived him as being "full of it". Lesson learned: Don't make assumptions about your customers (or anyone for that matter) before making an effort to get to know them. You have to connect with your customers on a personal-professional level to understand their needs.

However, the Mister Ds out there do not have a legitimate reason for being one of THOSE customers. Although they are in the minority (luckily), there will always be customers that make the THAT-customer-list just because they choose to. Let me introduce you to the second Mister D, the new lodge manager. I dealt with this guy when I was team leader of a technical department. As a new lodge manager, he had swapped rolls from IT support to IT customer. He had actually been working in some sort of IT services delivery all his life before he joined the lodge. He understood IT. He could help himself IT-wise.

One day his company bought a small printer from the company I worked for. The lodge is situated in a very remote part of Namibia. We couriered the printer to him. He connected everything and setup the printer. About a week later he phoned me to setup the scanning function. This is a ten minute job which I could easily do remotely. Upon my appeal to him to do the three or four clicks to get me connected remotely, he refused to do so. He said he has been on the receiving end for long enough during all the years he did IT support. So now it was his time to be on the dishing out end. He was not willing to help me.

Here you sit with completely irrational behavior. I had not done a bad job. I had not missed a deadline. I had done absolutely nothing to offend this customer. This Mister D had a personal agenda. He wanted to be difficult for the sake of being difficult and therefore acted completely irrationally. You cannot fix this type of customer. Mister D in this case was the only one that could fix the problem and that had to start with a change of heart on his part.

Furthermore, he didn't just refuse to help me. He insisted that I went out to do the job onsite. The lodge, by the way, was 428.2km from Windhoek. That would mean an 856.4km roundtrip of which half was gravel road, to do a ten minute job, on a printer that had been purchased on a cash basis without any form of service level agreement. Is this type of customer a "fixable" one? No, it's not. Should you avoid such customers because they choose to be unfixable? No, not necessarily. Is it possible to have business relations with this customer? Yes, it is. I will tell you how in the next section.

Now you might ask why you would tolerate this type of customer. The answer is for the simple reason that this type of customer's N$1 has the same value as the good customer's N$1. As long as you can handle these types of customers and not allow them to bully you into doing things that will make you lose revenue, you need to keep them.

HOW DO I FIX THAT CUSTOMER?

There are two ways of fixing THAT customer. Remember we have identified two types of *that customer* in the previous section. The method you apply depends on the type of customer. Some customers are fixable. You fix them by getting to know them so that you can understand their situation. The other customers are not fixable and they might not want to be fixed. You cannot fix them by building a relationship, but you can handle and maintain them by being strictly professional.

Let's look at the first group. In chapter 2 we talked about not taking it personally. This is how you handle the first kind of Mister D. You cannot understand a person if you have not walked a mile in their shoes. Believe it or not, but the majority of people in this world are nice. They want to be. Most people don't like conflict. So don't think all customers are out to get you. Don't make it personal and about you. It is your task to get to know your customers so you can understand them better. Ask questions. Look for signs in their offices of what their interests are. Is there a photo of your customer posing with a primary school soccer team? Does she have a certificate of appreciation from the Cancer Association on her walls? Is there perhaps a collection of die-cast car models sitting on his cupboard? All these articles are potential connection points that you can use to start a conversation.

Even if you have to literally bleed to connect with the customer, you could do it. This is what happened at one of our customers back in the DMS days. One day a customer phoned our offices and told us our technician was lying on the ground next to the machine sleeping. Obviously something like that was unheard of and we immediately investigated. We found our most senior technician there on the floor, luckily not sleeping, but passed out. This guy couldn't stand the sight of blood. He was busy repairing a high volume printer and accidentally cut his finger on the sharp edges of the frame. Obviously he did not intentionally bleed to specifically fix the customer, but we capitalized on this humorous situation. We used it to our advantage for months after the ordeal to build a closer relationship with that customer.

Always be on the lookout for how you can relate to and draw closer to your customer, especially if they're on the *that customer* list. Connect with your customer on a personal level. Always remember that you are a professional working with a customer. Don't get *into bed* with them. Never overstep your boundaries, no matter how comfortable your relationship becomes.

When you nurture the relationship with a difficult customer, you will soon find THAT customer becoming YOUR customer. This is exactly what happened with the first Mister D that I talked about. He went from being the customer that I never wanted to go to, to the customer that sought me out when he had a problem and the customer that I actually enjoyed going to.

We had similar customers at DMS. I cannot recall exactly when we got them onboard, but these guys had been buying equipment from us ever since I could remember. The business had two owners that were some of the most stubborn people I had ever met. Every three years when they upgraded their equipment, we would sit around a boardroom table and hear how we could basically do nothing right. They would dispute every single point on the proposal. More than once we would walk out of the meeting thinking that this time around we're not getting the deal again. They would often also threaten to take their business elsewhere, but time and again they signed with us. This is a good sign. It means you are doing something right. It means you are giving them something they cannot find anywhere else, even though they won't admit it.

You will always have THAT customer. Get used to it. The only thing that really distinguishes them from the other customers is that they are a bit more adamant about service. Why not give it to them?

There is another magic trick I want to teach you. It is simple, but it literally amazes every customer. It is something unexpected and it is something very few of your competitors do. It is a simple after-sale phone call. Whether you repaired a washing machine, delivered a cabinet or served dinner to a

customer, a phone call the next day works magic. Your customer will appreciate it tremendously. It creates a personal connection. It gives you the opportunity to have a normal conversation with your customer, unlike the usual phone call where he complains about his new problem. If you happen to be in the vicinity of your customer a week or two later, just quickly pop in and ask him if he needs anything. Just a one minute courtesy call like this buys you a lot of goodwill with your customer.

Let's now look at the second group of THAT customers. You will find that not all your customers can be charmed into a personal relationship. You might have tried everything. You tried connecting to him on common grounds. You tried with follow-up calls. You do weekly courtesy calls. You even threw in freebies with his sales, but nothing works. That is fine. That's the way it is, so stop chewing your wrists about it. Remember it's not personal. It's not about you. It's about the customer. The way to handle this type of customer is strict professionalism. Don't be stone-cold to the point of being rude. Greet the customer. Smile. Be nice. Just keep on delivering excellent service.

Keep everything on record. This is very important. You must always have the relevant documentation and correspondence in writing as far as possible. Details on contracts must be correct. Contracts should be signed and initialed on every page. This is standard business practice for all customers, but it is critical to have this flawless for THAT customer that you cannot turn.

I learned this from one of my employers, but it holds true for a customer as well. I used to work for a company where there was always something devious in everything the employer did. It was one of those situations where the MD and the owner of the company were personal best friends. So my word could never overrule the MD's word. The MD often had these spur-of-the-moment ideas. I call them Cowboy moves, because he would come up with an idea and we would all have to go in blazing guns without any planning, hoping for the best. Whenever a project worked out for good, the MD would take the praise for it, but when things went sour, he would blame it on someone else. I kept my professionalism, but I firmly demanded all verbal orders from the MD to be sent via email. That way I had proof if something went sour. He quickly learned that he had to be authentic when it came to dealing with me. However difficult or demanding or arrogant a customer or a boss is, he cannot argue away physical proof. Stay professional. Be friendly, but make sure you have your facts straight.

ON THE RETAIL FLOOR

The game changes quite significantly when you need to fix THAT customer in a retail environment. None of the previous tools can be applied on a retail floor, but the principles remain.

Whether you are dealing with a difficult customer commercially or in retail, the concept of serving others still takes mainstage here. You have to serve and attend to the difficult customer, but you should also be serving your employees simultaneously. Why do I say that?

Let me tell you about a hamburger takeaway shop in Windhoek. It was operational for just about a year from the day they opened to the day they closed their doors for the last time. After its first two to three months of opening it was said that they had the best burgers in town. It was a very small outlet that could fit at the most ten customers in a queue inside, but often as you came around the corner, you could see the queue extending out the door for about another fifty meters. Those were good burgers!

The layout of the shop was simple. The customers actually queued in a kitchen style room. The grills and preparation tables were actually what separated you from the chefs. It was always very noisy with all the commotion. Patties and tomato slices and sauces would fly all over the place. Yet, it was an enjoyable experience watching your burger being prepared before your own eyes. It tickled the taste buds as you anticipated that first bite.

One day I arrived there to find a new manager. He was just as vibrant and loud as the previous one. He was just as hands on yelling orders to and fro. Yet, there was a distinct difference. He was one of those types of retail environment managers that would serve customers at the cost of his employees. In the name of good customer service, he would sacrifice serving his employees. If something went wrong with an order, he would scream derogatory comments to his people. His attempt to portray good management skills and good customer service skills actually left a bad taste in your mouth. The retail floor is not the place to reprimand your staff.

Do not get into an argument with your customer on the retail floor. If possible, invite him to your office. Offer a cup of coffee. Give him personal attention. That is what many angry customers need in a retail environment. Making them feel special will solve 50% of the problem immediately. Personal attention says they don't need to stand in a queue. It says they're not just another number. It says they are getting special attention above all the others. When you've resolved the issue, assign a dedicated person to the customer. That way you give the customer "special treatment".

All floor staff should wear nametags. It enables the customer to work with a John or a Jane rather than a guy or girl on the floor. It gives the customer's experience a personal touch because he/she has the chance to come back to John and Jane.

> *You will always have THAT customer. Learn to deal with it.*

CHAPTER 6. PROCRASTINATION

"What does procrastination mean? Never mind, I'll look it up later."

What is Procrastination?

The best definition of procrastination I have ever heard was recently over the radio. The guy said, *"Procrastination. What does that mean? It's alright, we'll look it up later."* That is exactly what the problem is with procrastination. The keyword is *later*. The project is due only at financial year end, we can do that *later*. The exam is only next week, I'll study *later*. Stock take is only in two months, I'll sort out my negative stock *later*.

Procrastination is not just putting off certain tasks. It is also putting off higher priority tasks because you don't like them and prefer doing the lower priority, more fun tasks. Whichever way you look at it, there are three consequences of procrastination. It causes major health, financial and relational problems.

Another form of procrastination relates to over-planning. A few years ago I was involved with a project in a field that was fairly new to everyone involved. The MD of the company was also closely involved in the project. He had the most experience in the specific field. We researched different implementation methods. We looked at different options. We planned and we had meeting upon meeting. We had brainstorming sessions and workshops. After a year and a half of planning, there was still no execution. We had explored every possible option and scenario that could potentially play out. There was no more planning we could possibly do.

The only reason we eventually got going is because this MD resigned. The project was launched after he left and of course it had its challenges like any other project. The theory and practice never aligns 100%, but there comes a time where you have to start the engine and see what happens. Do not go blindly into something for the sake of not procrastinating, but at some point you need to start. If you wait for everything to play out perfectly on paper, you'll never get started. Over-planning is counterproductive.

Being too dynamic is also counterproductive and can lead to procrastination. In today's technological age we have to be dynamic in our businesses otherwise we will not make it. The balance should be right though. Do not try to implement too many new ideas too soon in your business. Current projects should be finished first before another starts. Otherwise you will confuse your team, they will be overworked, and they will default to the tasks they are more familiar with, that are easier to do and that are more fun to do.

EFFECTS OF PROCRASTINATION

Back in my early days when I was still the technical Knight, I would start my Monday mornings this way. I got to work just before 8:00. On my way to the canteen there were about twenty minutes' worth of stops to talk about various weekend activities and sport results. When I arrived at the coffee machine it would be around 8:20 to 8:30. Then it was coffee time where the sport chats would continue. Any form of real work would only start after 9:00.

We had a bad habit back then of not doing much on a Friday. Although we were officially on the clock until 17:00, we would get into weekend mode from around lunch time. If the customer did not shout loud enough on a Friday, we'd postpone any new calls until Monday. The combination of postponed calls on a Friday and my normal daily postponed starting time on Mondays often led to problems for us.

The customer who was waiting the whole of Friday for either his products, service or quote, would often be up in arms by then. The customer whose Monday started with a broken office PC or printer wanted attention right away. You ended up doing crisis management and fending off everyone. There were excuses of how busy we were and how short-staffed our company was. All we did was put out fires. No wonder we always had a blue Monday. We set ourselves up for it.

The first thing procrastination does is it affects your personal health. Let's face it, procrastination is just prolonging the inevitable. You have to hand in that financial report, whether you like it or not. The exam date will eventually come and you'll have to write it. Procrastination does not eliminate the task you don't want to do. It just makes it worst. As the due date draws closer, the stress levels rise. This can lead to all sorts of health problems in the long run.

It dampens growth and creativity. When the due date is around the corner, we get stressed and we tend to default back to what we are familiar with. Last year February, during my studies, I managed to get a date for an assignment completely wrong. Purely by coincidence I had a look at the due dates again on a particular Friday. I saw that my 5000-word essay was due in three days on the Monday and not a month later as I had thought. I had the right day, but the wrong month.

Over that weekend I worked through a study guide from scratch and I submitted a 5000-word essay the Sunday night. After a lot of stress, very little sleep and lots of coffee I had made it. Obviously the amount of time I spent on the assignment was evident in the marks I got. Upon reading it afterwards I saw how it had no depth. It had content, but didn't say much. I didn't think things through. I didn't learn anything with this assignment. It was not procrastination that put me in the situation. It was an honest mistake, but the outcome was the same though. Leaving things till the last minute produces bad results. It takes away the focus from delivering something extraordinary. It only focusses on completing the task on time.

Good service delivery has no room for procrastination. It is a cancer eating away at your company. It does immense damage to your brand. It can do irreparable damage to your reputation. Customers do not want last-minute responses.

They will allow exceptions, but it shouldn't be a habit. Last-minute responses do not allow any room for error. If there is no room for failure, it greatly increases your failure rate. Last-minute actions are what makes you forget about adding the installation charges to the quote. It makes you fit the part incorrectly causing a premature failure. It makes you submit the financial report with flawed formulas.

Ultimately procrastination causes a loss in revenue. Procrastination leads to bad service and that leads to losing customers to your opposition. This results in a direct loss of revenue. There is another indirect financial impact that most managers and companies do not realize. That is the loss in man-hours. A 2011 study showed that 25% of daily work hours are wasted as a result of procrastinating staff members. Consider your payroll bill for a minute. You could be wasting 25% of that amount due to a procrastinating workforce.

There is no room for procrastination in a lifestyle of service. It is a counterproductive, revenue-eating, reputation-damaging cancer that needs to be eliminated from your character and company. The same study mentioned before, also found *high levels of procrastination is associated with lower salaries, shorter durations of employment, and a greater likelihood of being unemployed*. Procrastination gets you as individual nowhere in life and empowers your competition to take away your business.

SOLUTIONS

The number one solution to eliminate the cancer of procrastination is planning. You have to plan your days, weeks, months and years. What is it that makes you dive into the books the day before the exam? It's the exam date, right? It's the project's deadline that makes you work 24 hours non-stop, because it is due the day after tomorrow. There is no better motivator than a date that is slowly but surely creeping up on you. We are continuously in a race against time. We have to manage it.

Deadlines should be manageable. For bigger projects, split it up into several smaller tasks each with its own deadline. This way you will have manageable smaller tasks that you can focus on and it will give you a sense of progress as you tick them off towards the end goal. Nothing is more demotivating than continuously missing deadlines. It is better to set yourself realistic deadlines, firstly for your own sanity and secondly, which is even more important, to deliver on the promise you made to the customer. Never in my 20 years of dealing with customers have I ever met someone who was disappointed when a service was delivered earlier than promised. Rather build in an extra day or two as buffer than having to explain later why you missed the deadline by a day or two. There will often be unforeseen situations that are totally out of your control. These might cause you to miss the delivery date. Situations like these though are hardly ever something that happens at the last minute. There are always some sort of indication that a problem is luring. Keep your customer informed. Tell him about a potential delay as soon as possible. Last-minute excuses look unprofessional. Customers lose confidence in you, because it shows that you are not in control of the situation.

What is the next step after you have set out a plan for yourself? Nike has the answer for you: Just Do It. The best strategic planning in the world is absolutely useless if it is not executed. Often it is those daily, weekly and monthly repetitive tasks that are delayed. The irony is that these tasks are non-negotiable. They absolutely have to be done. So why prolong the inevitable? Take the bull by the horns and Nike it. There is only one way to get started...you start! I cannot count the number of times I have experienced this with mundane tasks. The moment you just start with it you realize that it is actually easier than you thought. It gets done quicker than you anticipated. It's actually not that bad. Before you know it, you are done.

> *Procrastination is a company cancer. Early diagnosis makes treatment possible. Late diagnosis makes treatment impossible.*

Chapter 7. African Service

"Don't worry...TIA (This Is Africa)"

AFRICA, AFRICA'S WORST ENEMY

If you've been to Africa and more specifically to Namibia, you most likely heard the term TIA – This Is Africa. Don't get confused now. It is not a term used to welcome you to Africa. It's an excuse for the level of service you'll get in our country.

You arrive at our Hosea Kutako International airport. Your first stop will probably be anything from the car rental or the Bureau-De-Change to a curio or coffee shop. You find yourself in a queue of 10 people. It is a peak time of the day and there is one clerk behind the counter. As you get agitated, one of our locals are bound to say to you, *"Hey my friend TIA! This Is Africa."* We seem to be our own worst enemies. Anton Du Preez, a Namibian speaker and trainer on various FMCG concepts, always say, *"You get what you expect."* He couldn't be more right. We plant the expectation in the visitor's mind and into our own minds and then we give it to them. As Africans we have become complacent with living the slow life. *There is always tomorrow. Why worry? Relax man...TIA.* We have set ourselves up for failure in the service delivery sphere of things. We expect of ourselves that we'll give bad service and lo' and behold, we get exactly what we expect. The problem is that the tourist might not expect bad service, because he is not used to it, yet that is what he gets. He just has to accept it.

The problem is made worse by the tourist accepting TIA and just living with it. It is quite understandable, because he is here for two weeks on holiday. He is in a relaxed holiday mode. It is not his responsibility to fix customer service in our country. It's Namibia. It's the responsibility of Namibians.

OPPORTUNISM

In life it is always easier to blame someone or something else for the situation I find myself in. We have too many opportunistic people living every day looking for the next chance to blame someone else. This is not unique to Africa, but I believe it is more predominant in Africa than the rest of the world.

I am Namibian. I am African. I was born here. I have lived here for 40 years. My wife is from Namibia. My kids were born here. My parents are African. They don't know exactly when or how the Botes family ended up in Africa. To us, we are indigenous to Africa just like any other tribe. The only difference is that I might be white and my neighbor might be brown. Or I'm short. He might be tall. Then again, I have 10 toes, but so does he. I have 2 kids and he has 7. I could go on like this for 10 more pages. What I'm trying to say is that in the end we are all Africans. Of course we don't all share the same worldviews. But do all Canadians share the same views? No. Of course we didn't have the same upbringing. Did all Australians have the same upbringing? No. Can we all make choices? Yes. Do our choices have an influence on the outcomes of our lives? YES.

I speak from an African perspective in an African context, but the concept is universal. You decide what you do with your life. For sure your history plays a role and it could have given you some sort of advantage (or disadvantage) over the next guy, but going forward, you decide what you become.

You will find a good example of making the right choices in a guy like Foreversun who grew up in Namibia. He was exposed to alcohol at a young age. He picked food from dustbins. He was involved in crime and fighting. He was destined for either a life behind bars or an early death. He was dealt all the wrong cards in life. Yet, he decided to get an education and today he is a motivational speaker. He works for the non-profit organization Blue Cross Namibia where he makes a difference in other people's lives by advocating the prevention of substance abuse.

The flipside of the coin is also true. You will find a guy like myself who was dealt all the right cards in life. I had every single thing going for me. I had a good education, stable family and friends. In my younger days though, I had this laidback attitude. I had an opportunistic mindset where I allowed my skin color to depict my actions. I decided to jump on the white wagon. My family has always been fine. We've had a decent childhood. I mean, we're white and white people have always been fine. That's what I thought. I had no urge to excel in life based on my own efforts. I soon realized that I'd have to work to come out on top. Riding the white wagon was not automatically going to get me anywhere.

What does an opportunistic and TIA mindset have to do with

delivering good service, you might ask. I want to relate these two concepts to poor service. An opportunistic mindset gives me an excuse for my actions. It gives me an excuse for delivering poor service. It gives me the opportunity to back away from my own responsibilities. I cannot deliver good service because I am white – because I'm black – because I am being oppressed as a minority group – because my forefathers were oppressed. An opportunistic mindset is counterproductive because it looks for excuses all the time.

A TIA mindset does the same. It is extremely counterproductive because it qualifies me to give bad service. You are expecting things to be slow in Africa, so that's what I'll give you. *This is Africa* should be eliminated from our vocabularies. Africa has all the potential in the world to become excellent service delivery gurus.

EXAMPLES OF AFRICAN SERVICE

There are companies on our continent that have definitely grasped the idea of excellent customer service. They show signs of a lifestyle of service. They are at a level that can compete with and beat any other global company.

The first example is FloraNiche in Durban, South Africa. They are florists that take online orders and deliver anywhere you want them to. In the spur of the moment I wanted to surprise my wife with flowers during her recent visit to South Africa. This was 20 minutes before close of business the day before she returned. I didn't use the online order tool, but phoned them first to find out if my late order had any chance of being delivered that evening. For same-day deliveries, orders must actually be in before 13:00 and here I was phoning at 16:40. I was not too surprised or disappointed that Cariemah, the florist that answered my call, declined my request.

I was absolutely amazed though with what happened next. Firstly, Cariemah apologized. For what? She had zero reason for having to apologize, but she did. She didn't stop there though. She went further. She asked me for my wife's number. She offered to phone her, tell her about my intentions, apologize to her for not being able to deliver and told me to dictate what I wanted to write on the card, so she could read that to her. Eat your heart out all you non-African countries! THAT is service.

I want to define good service delivery from what I learned from Cariemah at FloraNiche. Good service delivery is not doing something expected (even if that something is good), but good service delivery is doing something for a customer that they didn't expect in their wildest dreams.

The second example is that of Pupkewitz MegaTech in Windhoek. They are part of the Pupkewitz group of companies specializing in light fittings, bulbs and any other electrical components you can think of. One of their sales persons saw a customer searching for a specific bulb and obviously not finding what she was looking for. This was not in one of their own stores by the way, but in a grocery outlet completely external to the Pupkewitz group. She asked for the customer's phone number. An hour later she phoned the customer giving her the price and telling her she could come in because they had plenty of stock. The customer was an elderly lady. She had mobility challenges and said she would come in when she could. The sales person asked her for her home address and delivered the bulb that very same afternoon on her way home, using her own private vehicle.

You have to bestow good service delivery onto your people. It is a culture that needs to be cultivated among your people. What your employees do is a reflection of what your company does. In the MegaTech example we don't know who the sales person is, but that is irrelevant. If you find yourself in Windhoek in need of a bulb, who is the first company you will go to?

Unfortunately, we have plenty of bad examples of customer service in Africa. On a daily basis I have to deal with two of the country's national providers of certain services. We don't have the luxury of deciding where we want to go when it comes to certain services because there is only one provider.

Just recently, I again had to handle a situation where the services provided to my company were offline for more than a week. It had reached a point where I was not prepared to except any form of excuse anymore for not having the problem resolved right that instant. There comes a time when I decide to get involved myself. It only happens in desperate times. Unfortunately, when it has reached this stage and I get involved personally, I go into overdrive mode. This does not mean I become uncivil. It just means I refuse to accept any form of excuse whatsoever and I firmly demand a solution.

Within the hour our problem was resolved. That is all we wanted at the end of the day. We needed those services restored to continue running our business. That is always all your customer also needs. They just want to continue doing business. Do not ever allow your customers to reach that desperate point where they have to start demanding your service.

My ordeal with the national provider didn't stop there though. We had just gotten over the whole ordeal. I had just decided to let it go and not pursue it further. We were back online after all, but then a representative of the service provider phoned me. This was the guy I had been dealing with that day to get the problem resolved. I had expected an apology of some sort for the situation, but quite the contrary happened. He told me that they didn't normally charge a fee for these callouts, but because of my attitude, they decided to charge me. This is the kind of service that hangs the TIA (This-Is-Africa) name around our necks.

Whenever your service levels have dropped this low, you have to bite the bullet and do whatever it takes to win back a customer. Take responsibility. Admit your failures. Apologize. It is not a time to be arrogant and impose deliberate charges. It is not a time to become emotional and tell your customer he has a bad attitude. Your customer should never reach the point where a more senior person has to get involved to get a reaction out of you. It is your responsibility to respond to your customer's needs before it reaches a point where he has to demand service. In Namibia, when it comes to national service providers, the customer that is the most demanding and makes the biggest noise is the one that gets helped. Delivering service like this will not give you a sustainable business. Don't be like that.

Unfortunately for any service provider, I work in the service delivery industry and I have a great deal of experience in the field. I will not take no for an answer. I will be adamant about receiving the service I pay for. You should not allow your service levels to slip to where a customer becomes desperate. On the contrary, your customer should not have to think twice about doing business with you. When they hear your company's name, it should be a no-brainer to them. Your brand or company name should be synonymous with the service you provide. If you bake bread and anyone ever mentions fresh bread, your name should pop up in their minds. If you are a plumber and someone's drain is clogged up, your name should be on their lips. This is what FloraNiche and Megatech has done to me. I will forever remember them. Do you need flowers? FloraNiche is your guy (or girl in my case). Need a bulb or light fixture? Megatech is your man (OK, again it was a girl).

SERVICE IS MONEY

A colleague from the South African office visited Namibia some years back. On our way to the airport to drop him off, he said something that I will never forget in my life. He said money is literally lying around in the streets of Namibia. You can open any business you can think of in Namibia and start picking up the money lying around by doing one simple thing; *give service*. He even went so far as to say you don't have to give good service. You just have to give some sort of service, because the slightest hint of it will make you outperform the rest of the market.

The Namibian market is far from a lifestyle of service. We have a great deal to learn from the rest of the world, but it is possible to change. It starts at home. It starts in your heart and in your mind. When you start delivering good service in your business, you'll see proof of it on the bottom line of your financials. Customers in Namibia are hungry for good service. Discounts only take you so far. Offering a wide range of products will help and your business' location is important, but in the end it is good service delivery that brings customers to your doorstep even if you are more expensive or you don't have the widest range of products or your business is not suitably located. Customers are willing to pay for good service.

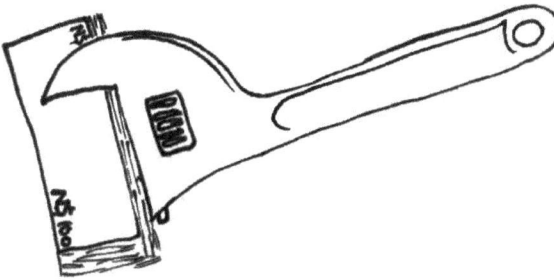

I recently dealt with a service provider that really delivered bad service. After a long discussion one day about his services that were continuously offline, he ended of arrogantly reminding me that he did not always charge us for his services. He made sure I knew that he had done a lot of favors for us in the past at no cost. He had no words for what I told him next. I begged him to please charge us for everything he did from then on, but to make sure his system worked. He was not expecting that, because he was using his apparent free service as an excuse for his bad service. Needless to say, his service levels has not picked up, the product he supplies still does not work and we are in the process of going over to a new provider. Customers will gladly pay you if you deliver good service. If you deliver bad service, even it is for free, people would not want to do business with you.

If you look for an excuse for your level of service, you will find it, guaranteed.

REFERENCES

1. Adam Pfau. Fixing uneven arms. Online blog. Accessed from http://pfaufitness.blogspot.com/2012/02 /fixing-uneven-arms.html, 13 April 2018

2. Biz Guru. Brian Profile and Thinking Styles. Online resource. Accessed from http://www.biz-guru.co.za/brain-profile-and-thinking-styles/, 13 April 2018

3. Caledonian Mercury. Private sector is no knight in shining armor. Online resource. Accessed from http://caledonianmercury.com/wp-content/uploads/2010/06/knight.jpg, 19 April 2018

4. Yashin-Shaw I 2018. *Leading in the Innovation Age.* Innovation Edge: Australia

5. Wikimedia.org. US Navy 040308-N-0000P-002 Sailors practice repairing leaks. Online resource. Accessed on 20 April 2018.

6. The Namibian 2013. A glimpse into the taxi industry. News article. Accessed from https://www.namibian.com.na, 23 April 2018.

7. Jon Geeting 2014. How many taxis per person should Philadelphia have? Online article. Accessed from www.planphilly.com, 23 April 2018.

8. Total Uptime Technologies 2017. Is the TCP/IP Protocol on the way out? Online resource. Accessed from www.uptime.com, 23 April 2018.

9. Ambitious About Autism 2017. Routines. Online resource. Accessed from www.ambitiousaboutautism.org.uk, 26 April 2018.

10. Harvard Business Review 2014. The Value of Keeping the Right Customers by Amy Gallo. Online article. Accessed from https://hbr.org/2014/10/the-value-of-keeping-the-right-customers, 2 May 2018

11. Ohorongo Cement 2018. About Us. Online resource. Accessed from http://www.ohorongo-cement.com/about-us/, 2 May 2018

12. Foreversun 2018. Foreversun The Namibian Story. Online video. Accessed from https://www.youtube.com/watch?v=SbPSj7vHkAg&feature=youtu.be, 25 April 2018.

13. Sophie Benne 2016. A Leopard cannot change its spots. Online article. Accessed from sobritish.eu, 7 May 2018

14. Nguyen B, Steel P, Ferrari JR 2013. Procrastination's Impact in the Workplace. Online article. Accessed from https://onlinelibrary.wiley.com/doi/abs/10.1111/ijsa.12048

ABOUT THE AUTHOR

Dewet Botes is the husband of Belinda Botes and they have two children. He was born in Windhoek and is a Namibian and African in flesh and at heart. He grew up in a small northern town, called Tsumeb.

Dewet has more than 20 years' experience in service delivery in an IT environment and more than 8 years' experience as trainer. He is a final-year Bachelor's degree of Theology student through the South African Theological Seminary. He is an EC Council Certified Ethical Hacker and an associate member of the Professional Speakers Association of Namibia (PSAN).

Follow Dewet on:

Facebook at www.facebook.com/dewetbotes

Linkdedin at https://www.linkedin.com/in/dewetbotes/

Twitter at https://twitter.com/dewetbotes

A Lifestyle of Service is not just another customer service handbook. It is a guide that will encourage you to live a life of service which will automatically bring about excellent customer service.

It is a book about serving people, whether they are your customers, your children, the waitress at the restaurant, the CEO of the bank or the homeless guy on the street. Serving others (society) can make this world a better place and serving others (customers) will grow profits for your company.

ISBN: 978-99945-87-59-9

9 789994 587599

Dewet was always available. He was always-on whether in or out of town. No question was ever too dumb or uninformed. He was absolutely trustworthy in our high security risk environment.
Ida Bouwer (University Research Co.,LLC)

Dewet is an intellectual, reliable and trustworthy person. There was never one day where he indicated a customer was too big or too small for him to handle.
Carl Sass (Cosmic IT Solutions)

Dewet is a reliable and trustworthy person. Appointments were followed strictly. There was never a day where your query or problem was too big or too small. You could always try your luck with a call-out, he somehow made time to pop in. He made life easier for IT related matters.
Harry Hanstein (Bank Windhoek Financial Advisors)

Dewet Botes is the husband of Belinda Botes and they have two children. He was born in Windhoek and is a Namibian and African in flesh and at heart. He grew up in a small northern town, called Tsumeb.

Dewet has more than 20 years' experience in service delivery in an IT environment and more than 8 years' experience as trainer. He is a final-year Bachelor's degree of Theology student through the South African Theological Seminary. He is an EC Council Certified Ethical Hacker and an associate member of the Professional Speakers Association of Namibia (PSAN).